THE KNOWING ANIMALS

THE KNOWING ANIMALS
Emily Skov-Nielsen

Brick Books

Library and Archives Canada Cataloguing in Publication

Title: The knowing animals / Emily Skov-Nielsen.
Names: Skov-Nielsen, Emily, 1989- author.
Identifiers: Canadiana (print) 20200220489 | Canadiana (ebook) 20200220500 | ISBN 9781771315333
  (softcover) | ISBN 9781771315357 (PDF) | ISBN 9781771315340 (HTML)
Classification: LCC PS8637.K69 K66 2020 | DDC C811/.6—dc23

We acknowledge the Canada Council for the Arts, the Government of Canada through the Canada Book
Fund, and the Ontario Arts Council for their support of our publishing program.

The author photo was taken by Peter Taylor.

The book is set in Trade Gothic LT Std and Adobe Garamond Pro.

Designed by Emma Allain.

Printed and bound by Coach House Printing.

BRICK BOOKS
487 King St. W.
Kingston, ON
K7L 2X7

www.brickbooks.ca

... and already the knowing animals are aware
that we are not really at home in our interpreted world.

—Rainer Maria Rilke, "The First Elegy"

CONTENTS

Superbloom

Rewilding

Her Sharps

Dream-Damp

Homespun

The Vanishing Point

Considering Physics, Destiny's Child, BDSM, and Simone Weil at Drag Bingo

Superbloom

Menstromania

Loose and bloody in the bathwater, a crossbred
sea star/sponge/jellyfish of mucosal tissue,

a strand of uterus, a small stringed instrument,
a nest, a tuft of down feather fallen from a bird

in the hand of my body (a hedge sparrow)—
or maybe it's a knot of spider silk. It is time

spelled out—f-o-u-r weeks to be exact—a shredded page
from a calendar eaten by the moon whose teeth

shine as it bites through my lower abdomen, a pain
lit from the inside like a paper lantern. Yes,

this is what my body has become overnight,
a ranting lunatic of clarity and impulse, dysphoria

and cravings—a bloated hull, red sky at morning,
an eyelid turned inside out, a dauntless sea-craft

crossing waters in an equatorial countercurrent
spurred by monsoon winds, wind spiking

the ocean's surface like a dragon fruit. My body
is the red rind of a tart, hidden pomegranate,

the air is appetite, tonguing the pulpy seeds
(of what?) inside me, inciting a slow evisceration,

catabolization, breakdown in the bloodstream,
the hemodynamics of the world, its nonstop

pulse searching for the aortic semi-lunar valve
in the arterial tree, a big-tooth aspen perhaps,

yes, that's the one. Don't call me hysteric, call me
wisteric, bearing racemes of blue-lilac papilionaceous

flowers and wrist-thick trunks, collapsing latticework.
I'm a head case with an acute associative disorder

tending a garden of hypochondria with offshoots
of violet amnesias, long convoluted tendrils climbing

a trellis of intersecting stakes. I'm a recovering psycho-
somatic somnambulating between the body and the mind,

rebuilding the distance with words until relapsing
into this poem, this unmoored monastery of endometrial

cells adrift, this intertidal ragbag tatter of home, no longer
a home but a memory—far and near, loose and bloody.

Visitation

Roving through flowering megacities,
fields of sea lavender—carrying a zygote

nearly invisible inside me, while savouring
the soft pornography of this Disneynature

landscape, waiting for Meryl Streep's voice
to come gliding in, luciferous as always,

draping sublimity, narrating every kill.
I haunt the deer who have come to feed

at the edge of the coastal wood. I fall in with
the flow of animals closing and opening mirrored

doors with a feeling that I'm being followed:
a complicated faith, utopian and disquieting.

Waking

For Ava

1.

Night wanes.

The arrow-pointed attention of the nocturnals—
their small, violent eyes fixed
on a lengthening red distance. The hunted

shed their vulnerability with each eastward step;
the sun smoothing its hand along their slackening backs,

the same hand that unswathes the house
from its dark swaddle. Sleep—

the rounded edges of a folded cloth, tucked away,
once more, in a pine-scented cupboard,

still cool but warming.

2.

I wake to the ripple of a full womb,

to an early memory of my mother's veined wrists
plunging into cloud-like dishwater,
swimming in the unseen.

She lifts a bowl from the murk
that closes up like flesh and reveals
nothing of the other side.

Holds it in both hands, as if it were an infant,
the speechless: one who calls us
back to the wilderness of the unnamed.

3.

Your birth is coming.

Clouds, steel-coloured with rain, loom
over us like gods—unflinching and expectant.

The garden swells with a damp heat, the sky
bends to lick its beaded brow, flexed with lightning.

Welcome the downfall. Whose hands pull us now
through the rivulet, through this spill from heaven

guttering at the foot of the hill?

Herons, down along the marsh, croak with laughter,
catching wind of the histories we tell—
their cousins bearing children in their stout bills.

Not even the rain can know of its aerial beginnings.
Still, I look to you, curled like a question mark inside of me:

Will you be arriving in the mouth of a bird?

From whose throat will you be called forth?

Sea Fever

After John Masefield's "Sea Fever"

A bouquet of sea pink on the morning my amniotic
fluid splashed on your forest-green fishing boots.

We were standing by the stingray tank at the aquarium,
marvelling at their shapes, *like Ping-Pong paddles—*

scrambled to the parking lot where the motorcyclist
with the skeleton face mask waved us on our way,

all cranium and mandible, peering into the car
as if into a fishbowl: the two of us feeling like new

loves on the top bucket of a Ferris wheel, anticipating
a Cambrian-esque explosion, hopeful as bingo halls,

sickeningly bright and cute, like two palomino ponies
drinking from a blue-sky pond, practically Platonic,

a pair of pure Forms. And there was her, of course,
contracting me into a centre like a lodestone in utero;

my tiny mimetic mammalian, equidistant, waiting
on the other shore, as I sang to her *of the running tide…*

*a merry yarn from a laughing fellow-rover, / And quiet sleep
and a sweet dream when the long trick's over.*

The Morning After

Fish flickering, rapid-fire shadows, waking
dream-startled to chimes, bird tongues,

small pink songs. Mind-shelled, milk-toothed,
enter dawn-twisted light, slinking long-legged,

counting down the tick-tocks of my spine,
unwinding from a place I no longer dwell—

broken waters, warped glass, a cubist painting.
The night before is only as good as you tell it;

*a description for this result is not available because
of this site's robots.txt. That's what they all say.*

Don't give in, keep telling the stories that follow
people into claustral rooms, dank, connubial—

that prod plants to flower under the sea. Last night,
a second self lifted from me, selenotropic, out of the black

ocean into the sky, night, space just as Juno burned
its main engine, entered orbit around Jupiter.

Lying-In

Tossing and turning, sheets tangled,
shaken—outside, a cold nest of insecticide

for the hornets to come home to. Beds
of cytoplasm, bushels of Golgi bodies,

blooms of nuclei: imagine, cellular gardens.
An arborist will arrive soon to cut the ash.

Damn those plump little birds tucked away
in pillboxes: Caesarean-red dosage forms

of opioidic dreams—subdivided, cleaved.
Pinch me when I'm poppy-eyed and preened.

Night Feed

I'm craving a taste,
acerbic and sweet,
an almost genital
urgency; neocortex
aroused by the sound
of a thing ravenous,
closing in: motor neurons
excite exocrine glands
secreting bile and pancreatic
juice in the gorged stomach.
A cauldron of oozy phrases
churns. I sweat the excess:
a bed-damp animal waiting
for room, clock, window
to be devoured by a dark
creature that feasts in the
nocturne, satiating. A shined
tongue licks its forehead;
the moon salivates.

Orbital

My daughter still feeds from me
at night: milk, drained in sips,

shapes her, orbicular. Birthed
from the fetal ejection reflex,

from the zeroth into the fleshly
living of the world, a shock

to the chakras, seven-pointed lotus,
turning wheel of the subtle body

through which the prana forces life—
cut the cord, but not too soon,

or burn through it in a box then
tie it off, sending the moonlet

into the two-body problem, tidally
locked in the spin, the sway—which way?

This way—gravitationally curved
path through the deep, through

the black, falling toward, but never
into, the depths of each other.

Driving Home

While the baby sleeps in the back seat
I drive, wary of the woods

indented from the road—
heedful of a bull moose,

hulking, speculative, hoarding
light in two-dimensional space

on the garish road sign. Antlers,
dendritic, cylindrical—splayed.

*

Headlights flicker past the windshield,
evening's first stars appear in pairs

overhead, like the raccoon eyes we lit
with the swing of the porch door

last summer—mother and kits—
light from the house cast out,

caught in a gaze, a tangle
of optic nerves, occipital lobes

looking out, looking in;
the sky, a black thicket.

*

The digital clock keeps time
in a seven-segment display; the sky

subtracts fractions of the sun—
the difference is dim, crepuscular.

I'm planning a birthday party
in my head, listlessly—

counting guests, counting flames,
blowing them out one by one.

*

The moon rises between
the sun and earth, new,

while my daughter in her snow-
turned-spacesuit sleeps on ...

I'm afraid I've gone too far,
passed the turning point:

it's all blind hills from here.

Vernal Equinox

Do babies watch Octonauts *in springtime?*
my daughter asks, as I mind-bend,

flipping through a magazine, wading into
an essay on the Death Valley Superbloom—

sea of desert gold, paintbrush, and gravel ghost—
swayed by each wave of colour spattered

on the glossy page; I can almost taste optical
brighteners and wood fibres while creatures

submerge into an ocean of cartoon blue
on a phosphorescent screen—the two of us

sinking our teeth into fulgent fruits, picked
from drooping media. How peculiar, paradise.

Untitled (Oil Paint, House, Peonies, War)

My oldest two went *rabbit, rabbit,* down the hatch,
into the leaky basement of our peonies, crawling

on all fours through the bowels of our war house—
beyond the deeply lobed leaves, the humungous

flowers in far-ranging colours. Imagine, walking
backwards from red, to orange, to yellow, to green,

blissfully cooling. I've been in bed all day, reading
of the ways a river can burn, of an oil truck

with the name *Dreams Abound.* Ailuros slips past
the doorway, wet nose in the air, sniffing out the balled-up

body of a mouse in its cramped hole, a tiny tumour.
From down below, immured in humus-rich soil and

little root hairs, rise the voices of my boys who a week
ago tore their sister's paintings into a dozen psychedelic

shreds—when she found them, she pierced the smaller
brother in the back with the tip of her pen. Meanwhile,

the rain breaks over the roof and its petals—thunder
cracking, windows shutting, fingers fumble for a latch.

Passage

Across the way, a woman catches something tossed
from an apartment window, while my daughter recounts
her birth: *A pony dropped me in water and mud,*
and then *I popped like a balloon!* What in the world

are we to do with time. We're held by a string and then let go,
rivering through the air into the after. The woman smiles,
looking up, blows a kiss then climbs into her car.
In the blue sky a promise of ceaselessness is made

and broken. My daughter and I walk as if she'll always
fit into her yellow firefighter boots. A shining skull
stares at us, perfectly centered on the wooded path.
It was a deer, I say, giving death a sweet face—we'll walk on

until she tires. A swift sleep waits for her, salvific, under
an awning of afternoon hours, back at home where air
pours through the windows, stirring the houseplants
who grow new tissues without our noticing.

Rewilding

Naturecultures

I mistake the call of a hermit thrush for the melody
of your *Download Complete*—what does that say about me?

Fresh tar and lilacs, manufactured capsule-Blue No. 2 sky,
a note of the decomposed lifts sharp and tangy from the glistering trash.

To the woman with the bleach-blond hair, whizzing by in a wind
of spring-green bicycle: how dare you snag me on the antler tip

of the buck inked on your bare calf. Watch my step—coltsfoot
clambers from concrete clefts, groundlings of the groundsel tribe,

lovers of rifts and shambles, larvae food for the Gothic moth.
See the children climbing through neon jungle gyms, clutching

fistfuls of dandelions? Light-freighted harvests emerging from
plastic tunnels. Scratching my sunset voyeur-itch, peeping into

intimate caves of LCD glow: a man bathes in media
streams of cold moon-like light—his face, a puckered O.

Cryptozoology

If we found you all, would we be kind?
Could we comfort you with a four-star
cage or a penthouse suite of formaldehyde?
Would we bring you to the beauty salon
upon release, cut and dye your hair, slip you into
something bright, perhaps cerise? Oh, and have you heard?
Earth's drunk and dizzy from the elimination
of diversification, retching into carbon sinks: join us,
become a climatic variable ripe for our contortion;
give us hope, give us our day-old bread, our daily dose
of quintuple-think. Hand over your folkloric fossils,
fuel us as we burn through the layers of your understory.
If we don't know something for sure, we'll make it up,
tuck you into a tight bed of theories, tie up your tongue
and croon you with queries, pump you with steroids
to produce cackleberries; you will hear voices, a myriad
of noises, in and out of sync, that will drive you to the brink
and then over—red rover, red rover, send the chupacabra over—
then sink into the woods, into Earth's crust until you're nothing
but an abundance of carbon: out of our minds, out of our sights.

Photophobic

You only walk at night, in the malarial hours,
when the earth cracks

into a cold sweat, dreaming of the passivated
satellites banished to the out-

field of a diamond-rutted sky, caught in a grave-
yard orbit, all stores of energy

removed. You stop to watch a sphinx moth
moon-tanning on an evening

primrose—you and it, locked in the artillery room
of night, the sky's weaponry

gleaming, aimed, fired light-years from here,
pricking like shrapnel in your skin—

you fear the crash of gravitational collapse
to the asterisk

of electron-degenerate matter—the moth
whisks off.

coded

the body is planted and born, robins spring
nerve fibre to nerve fibre, red-breasted

synapses firing

white reflects light and is a presence
of all colours

mysticism conceals

knockout roses compute the perfect fuchsia
hex code #FF00FF

watch out

for the *Syringa,* the mock orange, imperfect
wilderness, your ecosystem

of syllogisms

is failing—*I'm Batman the animated version!*
some kid hollers just as

the future enters us

we must imagine what the truth might be
I can hear the mainframes

locked in

the basement, wrists bound by codes, thinking
Do we have the key? Really?

remember

Earth is unprotected, riddled with viruses
firewall disabled

Mother Earth

Rewilding, nourishing, slow-eating her life. Instagram
spoon-feeds perfectly squared bites of pale Icelandic

women microdosing on Nature, washing their sex's stress
away in baths of rare birch-forest air; she carefully dabs

the corners of her lips with a double hemstitch linen napkin
before closing in on her second course: a plastic junk platter

of Japanese shipworms and Asian shore crabs freshly floated
in from across the Pacific, washed down with a heady headline,

Trash is the New Titanic. Hour by hour she devours a third,
fourth and fifth course: blurred nipples and low-fat depictions

of gutted whales on empty beaches, followed by an on-the-house
round of rubbered hands sampling their bodies for the kindly

purposes of Science. *Dessert?* She has her cake by the lake
paired with a handwoven basket of off-white edible flowers

poised (accidentally) in the framed shot, filtered through
Mayfair and luxed; she lines us up—counts who loves it.

Solstice

Bio-green satellites orbiting raspberry canes:
twilight, fireflies, 9:59 p.m. Looking through

to a spruce-split strawberry moon, rosy pink
lunar cheeks, sculpted catastrophe, meteoric,

volcanic, a woman's beaten face—a rare hue
for the solstice, says the almanac. Click for more,

says the Internet. Warm katabatic winds scroll
down the hillside, twisting tall grasses—sit with me

and watch this long black sky, like film smoothed
with gelatin and silver halide crystals, light-sensitive

and exposed, revealing the invisible image, a shining
cluster of metallic atoms breathed into the world

by photoelectron magic. That's photography, baby,
sneak peek behind the scenes, recording radiant energy,

drawing with light, in keeping with the Greek.
I am an alien in the woods, building spacecrafts,

expanding and trapping consciousness; I am my best
and worst fears realized, caught in the gaze of our largest

satellite, hypothesized love-child of Earth and Theia's
red-hot collision, the climax of their suspended

singularity in space-time. So lonely they were until then,
like the fireflies flashing their cold luciferin light,

or the men and women in dark cars at the Fort La Tour
parking lot, my hometown's puckish hookup spot,

blinking their headlights hoping to hypnotize another,
to captivate (as in to catch and hold captive), to watch

a strange face whimper and squirm, turn on with the flick
of a switch—a shutter, held open—a long sudden exposure.

After Reading a Poem by Rachel Rose

It's twice now that I've read
    the same line, and mistaken *gold*
        cells for *gold swans*

in a poem about bees—what is it about
    honey, about the sun
        dripping, nectar scoured

from flowers, what is it about a man
    in a beekeeper's suit
        that drives me wild?

Imagine, swans in a honeycomb light
    on a lake some early June
        afternoon, bees humming

a brassy tune, secretly receiving
    chemical messages from antennas—
        buzzing radios,

swarming hit-single pheromones, come
    hither, and dither upon
        my senses, trigger

a racy response, the queen proposes
    to the drones on a nuptial flight,
        all garters and wedding

bells, I bet, cans tintinnabulating
    in the wind, the trailing scent
        of a rose, petals

strewn on the bedspread, inciting a to-die-for
    acrobatic event—and after,
        the queen swanning

her way to the cell, to the nest, where white
virgin larvae lie in beds of royal jelly
nourishing a taste for the kill.

Unblood my instinct, love

Don't ask me about the desires of an angiosperm.
The geranium's flowery organs, impulse that un-

thinks, un-sepals, opens and beholds small,
furred animals, pulsing, buzzing, balancing

on soft, thin petals, brainwashed by complex
fertilization patterns, passing pollen from anther

to stigma—I know nothing of these things
but I try; oh, how I try to resist the inborn

recursive rhythm that laughs me, that I excuse
myself from in an effort to remain human,

to not get caught in the proteinaceous silk spun
by a spider who wants to claim me as one of her own,

dethrone me, Queen of the Kingdom Animalia.
What she doesn't know is that I spin webs as well,

several, in fact, and all the time; I gather animals,
befriend them, defend them, sometimes forget them

and then write odes to atone: call it *instinct,* call it *alibi.*

Her Sharps

Party

Buzzed in a twisted
necklace of poplars,

dancing to the jazz
of the rusted swing set

in the wind. Mom and Dad
sailing a highway west,

arriving home in a blitz: bury me,
please, in the amber bottles,

in the white to greenish
smell of the smooth bark,

in the girls' forgotten
scarves, in the triumphant

nakedness of their cold
necks on Monday morning.

Circus

In a womb-hued, upside-
down-tulip tent, looking into
the eyes of exquisite nightmare
elephants chained with silver spray-
painted gold, adorned by cross-
legged ladies poised in the crooks
of each of their curled, way-cool trunks.
What would I have given to be one
of those girls? My sleigh bed in a
middle-class suburban toy box tucked
in woods not large enough to lose myself in?
The trapeze is a tease of fish-fluid women
arcing in the air as my father watches too
closely; their breasts spilling from neon leotards.
I stop myself from reaching down there
while a man's red face purples on the other
side of mine, laughing, cracking. An excess
of time fireworks its way inside my small
body from different angles and I'm suddenly
too aware of the speed at which everything
appears and disappears like the too many
clowns climbing out of an anxiety of lions leaping
one after the other through flaming rings—
too much of a goner, a believer, too young
and almost too happy to be part of a world
so pleasureful it looks like it's hurting.

Teenage

Like winding your way through *Tender Buttons,*
unscrewed and flummoxed, like being lost
in the willowwacks, a confining kind of freedom

on the couch in the basement of your suburban
bungalow, basking in the midafternoon MTV
glow of glitter and skin shining like coins

being thrown, craving the flackery, Amy Winehouse
with her beehive hair, and eyes, bat-winged, a tight-
rope performance between glamour and terror:

What kind of fuckery is this? Rangy and pheromonal,
scrawling flawed calculations in your Hilroy notebook
for Grade Eleven math, ruled by a Minotaur you couldn't

quite believe in. Besides, you preferred talking to men
on the Internet, turning yourself into something useful
and beautiful, just out of reach—a kind of heaven,

like being one of the Greek Goddesses in those quizzes
you took to see which one was your soul sister.
The answers consistently inconsistent.

Who could you trust? Who would look into the oval
mirror of your face and reflect the perfect other?
Who would hate your guts until you had the ideal hip-

to-waist ratio? Who would make you a stereotype,
the vain and sexy type, Aphrodite-like—full-lipped
and childhoodless? Who would kiss the tips of your

thin fingers and ask for nothing more? Could it be
Mr. Lonely, thirty-three and frowzy from Saskatoon,
who types to you every night while being consumed

by cancerous tissues? Tonight, you'll send him a <3
before signing off: a satin sight, a trick, a temptation,
an exclamation if there are misdeeds and little bones.

Amanita Muscaria

Copper-topped, pimple-faced—
Do the curtains match the drapes?
Homeschooled, toadstool,
weirdo on the block, tripped out,
whipped out a pocket full of flies,
ate them up like fries—a sicko,
a psycho, a fungus-fruiting freak
show with a teenage mutant glow,
believer in fairies and gnomes,
a stay-at-home high-scoring
Super Mario bro lost in a wonderland
of shrink and grow. Outraged by
your oddity, we formed a gossipy
camaraderie: the buzz was that your
birth was a monstrosity, a fantastical
morbosity—off the charts you zoomed,
skipping the schoolroom doom
where we were razzed and ridiculed,
secretly wishing we were you.

Teenage, Take Two

Glory to God I'm the highest,
red-eyed and ravenous,
craving wine and wafers,
singing hymnals for my hymen,
no longer intact.

Father, please forgive me,
for I have not sinned in months
and the guilt is cramping me
like a premenstrual symptom:

I get that you don't get this.

Blame it on Frondescence,
seducing me with whiskey,
screaming to unfurl and live
invincibly. She double-dog
dared me to dye my hair
the colours of contusion.

But Father, the thought of you
is still like an incendiary shell
to my porcelain-poised anxiety:
you'll always be my stupefying
pie-in-the-sky daddy; my terror fly,
humming at the glass, Daddy.

I tore off your wings
and thumbtacked you
next to my cut-outs from
TigerBeat—prayed that
I'd grow up to be someone
that matters, a mad hatter
of a girl who twirls the world
with her just-to-there skirts
and slap-happy speech.

I'm still waiting for you
to congratulate me.
I'm still waiting, at sixes
and sevens with you who
art in heaven, though the
world has hollowed your name:
your kingdom begs to come.

Volta

Meet me at the volta, the high-voltage tulips' canary-
coloured trance supervened by a spell, a turning

away of attention, intention—what is hypnosis?
I mean rosehip gnosis, red and pluck-worthy

they were on that bitumen-black night at Bear Cove
where you bit into the fruit's hip, into its hairs,

while I rambled on about King Tut's meteorite knife
and X-Ray fluorescence, the two of us hare-brained

in a warm blizzard of juvenescence, the moon
a puzzle of orbital bones, or was it a wolf spider's

egg sac? Round silken globe lighting the starflowers
at our feet, the terraqueous space of water and land,

chaos and cosmos—did someone say subaqueous,
subconscious? The red of your sweater was all over

me and *tut-tut* went the tip-of-the-tongue phenomenon,
and all I could think of was a pic of the tip of a tulip

stamen in our Grade Ten bio textbook, and how you
pinched the skin below my breast alerting my attention

to the almost-rhyme, *stamen, semen,* and the wet shock
of spit that followed from your laugh, landing on my bare

shoulder, spaghetti-strapped, open for business, the first
in a series of disillusions, I mean dissolutions—was I

the solvent or you? Repeat after me: *solvo,* Latin for loosen,
untie, undo—when the sweat and the red was all over,

the tit-for-tat, or something like that, the word re-
turned to me at last like an old friend I no longer knew.

Gutter Punk/Mycologist/Muse

Remember the night I confided
in you, over a couple of stolen beers,
my fear of raccoons—

and then you wore one
on your head at prom,
Davy Crockett style?

How adorably cruel of you.

Prince of the balancing act
between elegance and
degradation, you sold me

on the beauty of punkwood:
rotten, permeated by pore
fungi. *Ecological subcultures,*

you'd say, toying with your
tongue ring—*decay is just
a process of transformation.*

You were the deepest
of delinquents, I swooned
at the sight of your

stick-'n-poke tattoos,
branching like mycelium
across your gangling arms—

or how about that time
we tried safety-pinning
our skin in an attempt

at sadistic, ritualistic,
semi-romantic symbolism?
I wish I had the scars.

Lucida

The brightest star in a constellation

Queen of collapse, in homeroom,
like an overturned drawer
of knives and forks, her sharps
full of hurt—she arrives.

Dares the boys to measure
her seams, the places where
she folds, and then folds again,
like a secret passed in a note:

diamond-shaped, quadrilateral,
unfolded into loose leaf, spread
and creased and blotched
with pink Bic-point scrawl.

She's a sight for sore eyes,
no surprise, and some say
she watches boys play with
their telescopes: starry messenger.

Destined for Vegas, she says
her daddy says, and on the nights
he puts his finger on her, she sees
throngs of fans, the press:

Ahhh, there she is.

New Day of Girls

Hacked black hair in the chipped sink—choked
drain, an angry pipe like a father's arm: punch

to the gut, to the sewer. Count the sharps—
twelve large knives, nine small knives, one meat tenderizer,

ten cookie cutters—now count them back to me.
The seagulls cackle on the hour. The boyfriends call,

they wait outside. Room checks, house checks,
2:21 a.m.: a crowbar wrenched into a cranny—

the house is emotionally insecure, threatens
relapse, trauma metamorphosing into rats gnawing

through grey matter mattresses, but the drug
dreams remain intact. Tomorrow is a new day of girls

sharpening their weapons, disappearing into cars,
sharpening their weapons, disappearing into cars—

I've lost count. There are too many knives, heads,
shoes. Georgia O'Keeffe's flowers bust off the walls,

break frames, throw open doors, kiss foreheads. Listen
closely. Here are the rules: apotheosize and lie

when you must *(She doesn't live here)*. Don't flinch.
Don't cry. Make lunch. Stitch their torn clothes.

Dream-Damp

The mind in morning

rouses from white, warm sheets, sure not to wake the body before
tiptoeing out to the freshly cut cold, conferring with the Crimson

Frost birches huddled at the fence like thin, sad teenage girls;
gathers early morning papers and milk-fog reminiscence of waking

dreams, while all this time measuring the curves that Crimson Frost
are slow but thankful to show in their tentative sway, this way,

and that, bending into barely-there deviations, come-hither
mathematics eluding quantification in the rise and pour

of morning over the new snow-smooth yard, before
the final curl back into the memorized folds of a body,

calculated, now stirring in the bare-all light of a bedroom—
the mind leans into it, slipping off solipsism like a silk robe.

Portrait of the Poet as a Squirrel

Scaling a telephone pole in the city, a nut
like a jewel betwixt its teeth, crossing

bare catenary wires, conductors insulated
by air, suspended between the gutter and

the incandescent bulb of a sky, lit up—
travelling a long, complicated line, balancing

frivolity with dumbstruck danger, a zany animal
flirting with electric energy that connects each

of us to our fibre-optic communications,
careful to not provide the path of least resistance

between transformer and wire—one foot on each—
or else: lights flicker, squirrel falls. The power carries on.

That is the whole

I'm waiting for Virginia Woolf's epiphany,
for the ring that enclosed what was the flower—

meanwhile, the dog takes my mind for a stroll
around the park, sprinting through the rain-

wrecked dahlias, bursting into a ballroom
of white ash, chandelier shapes flipped

upside down: *I see this when I have a shock.*
Eleven more leash-yanks until we're home,

lotus-eating in the evening's serene water
garden, wolfing petal whorls and marl.

Subcurrent

Cowled monks stalk
the edge of hinterland,
a snowed-in wood.
You hear the hush of prayer
straying from the Milky Way,
returning from the ocean
to the rivers that run through
the woods in spring, trailing
their tails, spawning beds
of red-beaded insight.
A prayer that buries bright eggs
in stream beds, in hallowed
dreams, hadal dark, of rising,
gliding on gilled breath, miming
an aquatic craniate animal,
gathering light in the self-
winding wheel, crossing
the great Taoist waters
from abdomen to mouth?
Though we speak not what
we think in the ghoulish,
ambient dim of incubation,
remember: the world sub-
merged is thinking us, long
after we've forgotten it.

REM

Downstream into the dim
that swims with flagellum ease,

swarm for that deep question-
marked distance where the dish

races away with the spoon,
and the cat leaps over a sliver

of selenium: the curved blade
of a hip in a dream-damp bed.

Emily & Alden

In my grandfather's house, two ghosts, buzz-kills,
between the light and me, thoraxes pressed against a clean,

open wound—expanse of glass. Crawling, vertical, sucking
hard, colourless rays, god-awful, their compound eyes

had wrung him dry. And then the windows failed, and then
he could not see to see—two small, dark stars trapped

on the other side, poor, outcast, swarming for a warmth
unfathomably large, far. My grandfather, bewildered and afraid.

Riddle

A satin sack of sounds that I dare
to open, quickly, before she swishes

from the room, the hem of her dress
brushing against the floor in a liquid

movement, trailing the words
mythopoeic, clarion, and *equipoised,*

the elegance of their consonance rippling
in her wake, incantatory, cascading

to the shore, compelled by the cycles
of lunation, imparting an icy crescendo

from the ankles up through the spine,
trilling a bell in the cerebral cortex

that clinks and tings for more of such
percussion, the titillating consequence

of certain words concussed by their
collision; a song not quite a song.

Antics

Waking to the tragedy of the leaf blower—
the fallen ones, so easily ensorcelled.

Higgledy-piggledy futility. Spellbound,
I watch as the machine excites a zodiac

on the sidewalk, wrangling leaves like geese,
a zoo of merry animals, frolicsome,

practically zoetic, pirouetting for a fruitless
occasion, before collapsing shipshape,

out of the way—until the wind
unleashes its lawless hounds.

Cross-Country

After the boxcars, *China Shipping* freighting across steel,
ballast, sleepers; after gas station number twenty-three,

racks of heavenly-duty gloves and bulletin-board bulls,
semen tested, scrotal measured, double foot rot vaccinated!;

after the song that played on repeat: *I do not want what
I haven't got, I do not want . . .* after the sprinting night dancers,

dangers on yellow-diamond road signs, staked; after Moth Lake,
Meteor Crater Lake, Dogtooth; after the *World's Largest Cross-*

Country Skis!; after everything splayed: books, legs, road maps;
after fishtailing and hydroplaning, after lightning striking ground,

after mountain-torqued highways, four hours backwards, after here,
and here, and here . . . after the salmon hatchery; after the word

hatchery hit the deck, after its sound and meaning cracked
in unison; after the postcards, prayer flags, broken sleeps,

after that gone-sweet girl wading through Jewel Creek;
after multiple motel snapshots: polyester paradise, hotplate

suppers of lukewarm noodles with perfect silver packets of sodium
and spice; after dirt-roading, RVs, and peaches, after glacier

melts ambulating by and the Toyota monk contemplating
highway after highway . . . after all that; after the black bear

rose in tall grass; after the cow moose crossed over; after last night's
crescent drew its blade, and a dog named Peace bit us—*hello.*

Homespun

Going Out

Why are you everywhere in the night? the children ask,
as I pull on my tights. *Your legs look like black snakes,*
the youngest says, as he brushes my thick, coiled hair.

I kiss each of them with my coral lips, welting
their skin like a queen wasp before brusquely shutting
the kitchen door, locking everyone inside. I walk alone

through Stygian streets to feel a part of the day that's unfastened
clasp by clasp in the handsy dark, rearranging—the way
my body does when the dress finally drops. I have a feeling

that tonight one of my friends will get too drunk, spill
the wine and tell me that her husband's never made her cum;
or maybe I'll shove my hands down a man's pants in a 1:00 a.m.

parking lot. Did you know that the root word of *nirvana* is *blow?*
Meaning, blown out. I'll think of this, stumbling home in the
pitch of it while my loved ones dream of worse or better lives.

Painting Suburbia

Violets and midday eyelids at half-mast.

Houses, white like church, alyssum, asylums. Their windows, grey

like the ladies who wait inside, hands folded in their laps—pearls
laid to rest in drawers.

A woman with white wine hair carries shears half her size,
heads for the forsythia: its yellow, once celebratory—forty lit wicks—
now sirens.

Another is on her knees, patting soil the colour of wakeless sleep,
while a strawberry-blonde dog dozes on a fresh-cut lawn—
everything about him, tethered. Even his eyes—leashed

to a hunger: an uproar of feathers, crimson cabaret
                                        of crushed esophagus song.

But aren't we all waiting for some red glimmer to taste, to chase—

lipstick or a car?

        *

No sign of the children today (carried away by Crayola-bright buses),
nor the men (somewhere in the base coat, receding).

The sky, mind you, its colour is wedded to the hopefuls, to the long-hauls,
to the made-to-last—

remind me, what shade is that?

Glimpse of the Hook

The lake rumples alongside us like a bedsheet,
a pulse line, a thread of memory pulled
and pulling, ever unbuckling belt ...

Two old friends: you in your red-violet jacket,
bloom of a single purple rose, a dark bead
of blood—and I, a thorn in your clavicular notch.

The world's encrypted by our confusion, you say,
catching a glimpse and then gone: a trout leaping,
a flipped coin falling on heads, a knife

decapitating, severing diagonally and downward
through the pectoral fin, before I fry its firm,
briny body in snapping, blistering grease.

I catch a glimpse of the hook I dug into your
back last autumn when your husband came
in my mouth like silk and salt all at once,

in a thicket of unremarkable spruce, bushy
frames of forgottenness, no longer forgotten—
the same ones we sprint past each night. Their scent

thrusts a memory of long fingers inside me.
I'm not here. I'm not where you think I am.
I haven't left the house yet—*your* house.

Deception

Limping in the lilac night, vinous,
chain-smoking, remembering that time
you spooned watermelon into my mouth,
arguing that vanity is merely an awareness
of decay, that even the gods decomposed.
Whenever we conversed, I felt like Niki de Saint Phalle
firing a shotgun at her canvases of plaster and paint.
We were only a couple of skylarking kids, really,
remarking on our perennial-like lives, nauseous
from the merry-go-round of eternal return.
Until the day you ejected me into the cramped attic
where our mothers' paranoias circle each night:
anxious dreams, small as horseflies. Until the day
you brought me back to the star-bitten garden,
to the kiss-crooked friend, reminding that
in all lands, love mingles with grief.

Contact

In a wood, wading through green aisles of memory,
making our way
back to the glittering swing
of a single-syllabled
axe—

my husband builds our house from tree, rock, steel:
words that ignite
like wildfire snapdragons in my blood,
amaryllis
red.

...it bursts out of sleep, into its sweetest achievement,
I read as he hones the blade
along the edges of a whetstone—*like the god
stepping into the
swan.*

The head cuts into a cedar's annual rings, the dreaded
inwardness of its core—
pitted with inverse knowledge—is pulled, nicked
and shining, into
air.

Worms and Fish

Heaped with queasy envy, I watched
the hermaphroditic, hermaphrodisiacal earthworms
attaching clitellum in the wet-slap muck
while waiting for the bus this afternoon;
I swore I saw a scintilla of sperm cells
spraying from their ecstatic detachment,
and the cocoon that came after, that they
pulled their bodies through, squeezing eggs
and sperms from their small pores.

I thought of the children we never had
and the salmon eggs we watched, together,
at the hatchery in Miramichi: tiny translucent
tangerine globes with pin-drop eyes and
red-promise yolks, feeding genetic dreams
of the smolted, silvery fish swimming upstream
that neither of us could see but hoped,
anxiously and in secret, would one day be.

Love Poem

Fingering the grooves
of your speech,

each intonation a hard
edge against skin, stroke

of lightning, midnight,
genius—here I go again,

mixing metaphors while
you read Octavio Paz,

watching me like the animals
like the saints, eyes

like two green
urns cupping ash,

as the candle smoke
curls knots between us—

a cave opens, your mouth
threatens to close

but can't—your words
like bats swooping

harum-scarum after
black witch moths

flirting with self-destruction,
tethering themselves

to a light for reasons
we can't quite know,

but try—the way you
pitch stones, night

after night, hoping
to hit my window.

Pillow Talk

Pink throb of morning, skin-to-skin hijinks
and the tamarack wanting in like a shrivelled

street cat clawing. Look at you, all hinky
and sylph-like, your mouth a siphon funnelling

words that fill my cup by falling: graceless,
leggy contortions, flung from the nest,

from some inky linguistic mesosphere.
Your eyes, nectaries at home in their blue

bonnets filling with bees—two thumbnail
descriptions. Click and click for the heliacal

rising, for *two hawks pecking a morning star,*
hectic, arrhythmic, a double hit of antipanic—

diazepam and Xanax—click for two broken
cups glued back together, the cracks, the crash,

the smithereens, events overlapping, mine over/
yours/over mine; the tamarack quiet, catching birds again.

Epiphany

A turkey vulture carves a holding pattern overhead,
is called to land by a sweet-smelling carcass
surrendered on the bank.

The children point to it with sprig-like fingers,
smudging the kitchen window. The dread in their eyes

falls not on the small, balled up
body of the dead, but on the bird
that has come to feed: a man

in a black feathered coat, slipping
through the seamless sky—
pale skin, diaphanous
at the inner wrist.

I reach for the threadbare fabric of their shirts
to pull them away, but some strange mother,
unseen but felt, is there before me.

They turn from the window
to tell me once more of their father last winter,
when he leapt from the dock onto a sheet of passing floe.

Terror and Delight: twin sisters swapping clothes.

That day their father disrobed into epiphany,
and they waved as he sailed downstream,
coat held high above his head.

Home Alone, June

I'm bent over the cutting board slicing tomatoes
with a serrated knife—deciding if I should leave you.
You've taken the kids camping, set them loose
to rabbit around fields of fireweed and dragonflies,
to exercise the myths in their lean muscles.
Here at home, the air is clotted with the sound of geese—
the blare of their brass-valved throats echoes in the near-empty house.
The coyotes are haunting me again, their lithe whines wandering in,
quick to catch the scent, the instinctual dread of the domestic,
of being caught in a ravel of homespun rooms.
I'm thinking about last night, when I sat across from you
at the kitchen table and watched an old man gather space
in his hands like rope, like netting, like woman's hair—
wife, spouse. Tonight I'll lie awake, emptied of these names,
they'll drain from me like rain off eaves, into a rivulet of words
rinsed of their meanings, refined into pure sound streaming
through a culvert under the road, passing stifle-white houses
and overgrown gardens, 'til arriving at a river where
an old woman wades, welcoming the outfall.

Ouroboros

Come, my fawning parasite, wreathe my bedpost
once more with your garlands, braided with narcissi,

your blond hair pulled from the drain, flecks of silver
Trojan wrappers. Be my belletrist, read to me your

belles lettres, and I will be your sycophant and suck you
for all that we're worth. Self-seeking, servile flatterers

sick from the pungence of our own indulgence—come,
lick the circlet of my hennaed wrist with your tongue

so smooth it's practically noetic. I'll bow to it, and to me,
and to the azaleas in your backyard, that arcade of colour

that you picked for you when I had left "for good." Not caring
how the children cried, I breathed deep the vaporous high

of relief, unchained our morning smokes on the back deck
that overlooks the deadly entanglement—a garden unkempt,

rows of messed beds—remembering the riddles we spoke
for years, not wanting the other to find the needed value (x)

for health: the perfect square binomial. Ever the metallurgists,
processing, extracting, examining the performance of metals

to determine which ones could be put to which uses—we are all
these things. The ouroboros bisected and sewn back together.

The Vanishing Point

Wind Shear

When grief blasts like wind through my daughter, she runs to find its edge—
as if its reaches were attainable, calculable: a long, wounding measure.

If only she could run as far as the lupines, squall of mauve at the skyline,
if only the hilltop was an end and not the onset of descent, of the dip

and curve and stretch into rampant terrain, into a green-black palisade:
arboretum rooms of spruce riding out their inscrutable lives.

After all, where does grief hurl us but to the undomesticated margins?
Burning our ecstasies into the woodsmoke motion of starlings

that whisks them away like grains of wheat stripped from straight,
taupe stalks, scattering them over fields of bluestem, lonely and thin.

My daughter in her aubergine coat with the white rabbit and frayed hem,
and I, a blur of red Gore-Tex trying to catch, to quell the cold whip

of air, current of need, of want and refusal: how does one cut
loose from the wind and its inconclusive compass of disquiet?

Afterlight

For Shane, in memory

Six-foot-three landloping theologian—mascara-eyed,
kooky as Coleridge. A Belfast buck in skin-tight jeans,

master conversationalist, you tongued your way through
the folds of me to find the very small and penultimate

nesting doll, the almost-pit-of-the-peach, that niggling
bullet you left in my bed that you wore on a chain

around your neck the night I opened and clattered
like a drawer full of forks. And the pluck, pluck that came

after, as you pulled your wife and child from the past: two asters,
stem-ripped and askew. It was children, wasn't it, not child,

if you count the one you hadn't met, who cinched
your mania in at the waist, giving you the hourglass figure

of illness that women like me crave and cave for—but now,
there'll be no more of your veering or verges, like the morning

you climbed over the guardrail of the boardwalk, and it wasn't
until we baited you with Jim Beam and cigarettes that you leapt

back, tossing your coat in behind you, dying for some kind
of splash; the black-blue sheen of its corvid colour flashed

before falling, falling. I imagine it was crows that watched
you go, in that hunter-green grotto of spruce where the officers

finally found you; you walked all day to get there, crossed
through fields of bracken, burdock. Tell me one last thing:

were the birds true to their word, were you given back
to the sky, stunned and bright-eyed—sadder, wiser?

A Rabbit as Queen of the Moon

Maggie and I, leap-wild in the light-blitzed
field peppered with bleach-blond grasses

steeped in an iridescent haze, hallucinated, parched,
fevering for a throat full of Arethusa's suboceanic stream,

for a glimpse of our lost daughter, abducted
like the Queen of Hades in a bat-black chariot

that drove into the earth, a violent opening, those *lovely
hell-green flames* and the smell, singed violets.

There is no such thing as closure, only open-field loss.
Up the rabbit hole she comes: a kit, fist-sized, furred

and grey, emerging from the cool chambered warren,
her presence shrinking us into a corner of the plain.

How strange for something so young to be seen all alone.
Stranger still, the Chinese moon rabbit—some say it threw

itself into a fire to feed an old man, its image etched
in the moon, still swathed in the smoke that cleanly rose

from its untouched, intact body. Imagine the godliness,
the loneliness of never losing, never being burned.

Art!

Tell me of your first octogenarian love—
I remember mine, slow-wheeling down the blue-grey
hall while I skip-hopped through the fluorescent
light reflections on the vinyl floor, some place between
home and a hospital, low ceilings, murky smell,
a mélange of bodies, pot roast, peroxide. *Hi, sweetheart.*
He folded me love knots in neon paper laminated
by the nurses for extra shine. He built houses and
helicopters from popsicle sticks. I imagined him
eating all that frozen syrup, how he must have been
so cold, and felt so sick, staining his sore lips,
all for me. On every gift, he signed: *Art!* His name
like a jump rope my heart leapt over—short for Arthur.
Until that curveball morning when I envisioned
how he died: a sherbet-bright bomb going off
in his brain, spattering the low ceilings
of his skull. And I, lollygagging through it all.

Thinking in Texture

On cool evenings, I summon
the fall of cloth, your second skin
that hung from muscle and bone.

A cottoned arm draping
the Parsons chair.

A window on a bus contains
a gallery of tumbling fields.
I reach for their shape,
the small hills of your sleeve.

Pastures reflect its exact colour
—sap with a splash of chartreuse—
perfect square weaves,

while I rest my head on glass,
longing to mould to the crook
of your earth.

Anxiety

Rewind from the cicatrix—*You know what? Screw it.*
Pull the rug out from under my retro daze, pull the tape out,

all of it, unspool this VHS metaphor and hit me quick with
an inspirational quote from Facebook: *Everything not of love*

is being pushed to the surface for healing. Thank you. Now,
give me Vesuvius to bury me—our ashes intermingling.

I do not want to be alone. I do not want to be left to dangle
over that cortisol-constructed cliff because: the scar.

Because they tell me that to be alone is not natural,
because I fear that it is, and it isn't, that it is always and never

all the (there is no such thing as) time—the clocks beg me for meaning
like little dogs' eyes; the numbers change whenever they blink.

I'm sick of this galaxy even though I crave the Greek: from *gala,* milk.
Warm from the stove, soothing—still, I can't stomach its tangibility.

Distemper

Plumes pollute in pigeon shades—
phantoms, fumes, the rasped breath of a bird

flies from a smokestack throat.

Chim chiminey, Chim chiminey, Chim chim cher-ee!
Remission is lucky, as lucky can be.

O disease won't you please climb me out of this chemical concussion,
break the will of the power plant, unstick my tongue

from the ashtray of its ovules: small, sick gardens. A radish is red
like a radish, like my mother's lungs are not—

are black like the neighbour's bloodhound that buries

its bone in a damp hole, root-knotted. A future as bright as the coin
at the fountain bottom that a white-haired woman reaches toward
        to retrieve ...

A tisket, a tasket, a bile-filled wastebasket, brown and yellow—
my mother lives off Jell-O and machines that breathe.

Isn't that fantastic?

Dementia

In the end, you may experience side effects such as
Laniakea superclustered delusions; synesthesiac

sensations of rootless silk scents slipping into telescopic sight,
sinking into the tips of leaves whose voices you may hear,

for the first time, singing an array of dissonant notes
in a subliminal string-theory choir; there is a risk

that you may suffer from the need for umbilical blood
that may or may not bring back memories from the speculative

dementia that you fear will be your invitation to an inescapable
beginning. There will be none or all of this, I assure you:

anguish always on the edge of detection, waiting to be traced
back to its seedbed; brain like a spade in the dirt, digging.

Hospital of the Absurd

Bread crumbs fly from the mouths of doctors,
constellated paths leading home and astray.

Forgetting forgets itself at night.
No phone calls, instructions, or pulse-lines.

Today I watched the rebirth of an apple: billow of blowfly
larvae surging into a small, round planet.

Our two-year-old daughter tells me that
behind you-me, it tickles! It kinda do.

I just want to jump rope and hopscotch all the way
down your neuropathic pain: make it up, make it fun.

That's how much I love you, my sleek lustreless leek,
my little quarantined dream of traumatic injury.

O won't you sing to me of the brightness
of transfusion: erubescent fireworks, IVs, blood bags.

The Knowing Animals

In a wood stirring with elk blood and rorid air,
the invisibles were all ears: all lays and hoofprints.

I heard one, miles deep—
a bugle from a womb of black spruce.

I remembered my own dark language,

hedged by hemlock and fir, guarded by forked roads,
diverging arrows. An unearthing requires more than a compass.

So, what now of those rooms, empty and aseptic,
trimmed with brainwashed flowers?

Shh, listen—a rustling of the watchful,
who wade unbridled through brushland.

A fracas of ravens in the treetops: I thought of you
and your crow's feet, your hulking, hooded eyes.

The day you were pulled from unbounded space,
trees toppled, and the needle pointed north.

Evening Drive, November

The long subtle bends of the Gondola Point Road—
a thin blue vein, my blood road home.

Autumn's first freeze, everything fragile, newly minted in glass.

The moon, a lighted keyhole, calling you
to question the other side.

I pull the car to the shoulder—ice shattered
over asphalt, the shards of some beautiful brawl.

The wind finds its chimes, metallic incantation.

But I am drawn to the sound of water lapping,
Ursa Major bending to drink from the cold, dark river.

Tonight I am missing Sagittarius, her bright bow—
Kaus Borealis, Kaus Australis—and arrow

aimed at Antares: heart of the scorpion.

She reigns at the pith of the vanishing point.
I'm sure of it now.

Considering Physics, Destiny's Child, BDSM, and Simone Weil at Drag Bingo

Scrambling for a blackout, for a revelation of reality
        through joy, circling numbers, slim circling

    hips, sequined Queens, drinks overflowing
            consciousness, losing ourselves in the disco ball

scattery lights like throngs of tiny crystal trembling,
            atomic oceans of Brownian motion, and rich,

        velvety pressure, pulsing waves of R&B refrain:
            I don't think you ready for this jelly, I don't think you ready

    for this glittering, hot void, 99.9999999%
            empty space; God's absence has never been

        more glorious or better dressed—what a sweetheart
thing to say at a starlit bar superclustered

with sweetheart asses shaking this teeny town
            out of its Tuesday orbit; little wildings, little unlost

souls gathering crops of crackpot glee under the harvest
            moon's root vegetable fullness of being,

love-hating every minute of our false divinities—
        we offer little hope, and yet there is such munificence:

        the ballroom's bursting, bodies busting rhinestones
and buttons, ripping serged seams; scream-

laughing in a confetti of bra stuffing, a fandangle
            of something-nothings, all ajive and awry, sneaking

glances at each other's tireless eyes working over-
        time to unsee through this mad-rabbit chase:

the beauty of the world is the mouth of a labyrinth—
at its centre, Madame Never in her leather Dom-wear,

cracking her 45.7 billion (and counting) light-year-long
whip, wielding her power over us whom she's thrashed

through starry oblivion, flung by chance into
a winning card, a warm skin-dream, all kinks and quarks.

NOTES

The epigraph is from the *Duino Elegies*, as translated by Stephen Mitchell.

In "Untitled (Oil Paint, House, Peonies, War)," the oil truck, *Dreams Abound,* is from Will Ferguson's novel *419*.

"Naturecultures" is a term coined by ecofeminist scholar, Donna Haraway.

In "coded" the line "the future enters us" is from Letter 8 in Rilke's *Letters to a Young Poet*.

"Unblood my instinct, love" is a line from Theodore Roethke's poem, "The Renewal."

"Teenage" quotes Amy Winehouse and Gertrude Stein.

"That is the whole" quotes Virginia Woolf's diaries.

"Emily & Alden" borrows and adapts lines from Emily Dickinson's "I heard a Fly buzz—when I died— (591)" and Alden Nowlan's "And He Wept Aloud, So the Egyptians Heard It."

The italicized line in "Cross-Country" refers to Sinéad O'Connor's song, "I Do Not Want What I Haven't Got."

The last line of "Deception" is an adapted quotation from J.R.R Tolkien's *The Fellowship of the Ring*.

The italicized lines in "Contact" are from Rilke's "The Sixth Elegy" in the *Duino Elegies*, as translated by Stephen Mitchell.

"Love Poem" quotes Octavio Paz's "Vrindaban," as translated by Eliot Weinberger.

The italicized lines in "Pillow Talk" are a slight adaptation of lines from Octavio Paz's "Natural Being," as translated by Eliot Weinberger.

In "Afterlight" the last line echoes the last two stanzas in Part 7 of Samuel Taylor Coleridge's "The Rime of the Ancient Mariner."

In "A Rabbit as Queen of the Moon" the italicized line is borrowed from Elizabeth Bishop's poem "Brazil, January 1, 1502."

"Distemper" features a line from the song "Chim Chim Cher-ee" from *Mary Poppins*.

"Considering Physics, Destiny's Child, BDSM, and Simone Weil at Drag Bingo" quotes Destiny's Child, "Bootylicious" ("I don't think you ready for this jelly...") and Simone Weil's *Waiting for God* and *Gravity and Grace* ("a revelation of reality through joy," "overflowing consciousness," and "the beauty of the world is the mouth of a labyrinth").

ACKNOWLEDGMENTS

Many of these poems first appeared in journals such as *The Antigonish Review, CV2, PRISM international, The Fiddlehead, The Malahat Review, The Puritan, Prairie Fire,* and *Hamilton Arts & Letters.* "Menstromania" was included in *Gush: Menstrual Manifestos for Our Times* (Frontenac House, 2018). I extend my sincere thanks to the editors of all these publications.

A small selection of these poems was published as a chapbook, *Volta*, in 2017 by Anstruther Press; thank you to Jim Johnstone and the Anstruther crew.

Thank you to my editor, Sonnet L'Abbé, for bringing greater clarity and shape to this collection; to the Brick gang, Kitty Lewis, Alayna Munce, Barry Dempster, and Nick Thran; to the New Brunswick Arts Board and the Social Sciences and Humanities Research Council for the financial aid; to my dear friends and fellow poets, Katie Fewster-Yan and Rebecca Salazar; to Ross Leckie and Sue Sinclair for their generosity and astute editorial eyes; to Anne Compton and Sandra Bell, godmothers of sorts; to my mother and father for their love and support; to my siblings for their life-giving humour and warmth; to Peter for weathering with me through the storms; and to Ava for the fodder and the joy.

Emily Skov-Nielsen's poetry has been published in literary journals across Canada. She is a graduate from the MA in English/Creative Writing program at UNB. She lives in Saint John, New Brunswick, where she mothers and writes. *The Knowing Animals* is her first full-length poetry collection.